# In Memory of Saaid and Aaliyah

*Two Angels Who Visited Us
for a Moment in Time*

AMIRA DAVIS

Olympus Story House
www.olympusstoryhouse.com

I was born Amira Davis in 1973, right after the Martin Luther King and Jim Crow errors were abolished. I was born in another era of time during the Black Panther Party when African Americans were still fighting for justice and equal rights.

My mother and father were a very young couple when they married and began a family. They were part of the Nation of Islam, following Elijah Muhammad, and were part of the Black Panther Party movement. When my mother and father married, my father also had an older daughter by another Muslim sister.

So, my dad had another baby on the way who is my big brother, Abdullah. I never met my older sister until I was fourteen years old.

I had an older brother besides Abdullah; his name was Saaid. He was the third of my dad's children, and he was brutally murdered at the age of two years old by my mother. My mother was charged with his murder and given six years probation, and the same day that they let her out of custody, they put us back in her care. I was born the fourth child and then was born the beautiful Aaliyah Davis. I have no memories of my older brother because either I was too small to remember, or my mother was pregnant with me. I was born after him in 1973, and then three years later, we had a baby sister named Aaliyah.

She was such a beautiful little chocolate girl, and she was just a beautiful soul. Aaliyah and Saaid were two angels who visited us for a moment in time, and I have not forgotten them. Soon after my brother died, my mother and father separated. Abdullah, Aaliyah, and I lived with my mother in a small apartment in Germantown, Pennsylvania.

I remember my brother Abdullah going to school; he must have been in the first grade. The bus used to come to pick him up, but I remember the abuse got worse when my father wasn't around. When he came to visit, everything was fine, but as soon as he left, my mother would be acting so evil. I remember one time she tried to stab me in the eye because she told me, and Aaliyah were going in and out of the refrigerator because the refrigerator was leaking water and she beat us really bad.

Soon my mother took us, my brother Abdullah, Aaliyah, and I. We lived in the Islamic community at Fifty-Second. I remember walking with my mother on Fifty-

Second and Girard, and my father saw us; they got into a fight, my mother and the Muslim brothers that were with her. My dad snatched me up, threw me in the car, and went to Baltimore to his parents' house.

My mom-mom and pop-pop were there; it was summertime. I remember being across the street from my grandmother's house playing with my little cousins. And I love their mother so much; I wish she was my mother, my beautiful Aunt Daisy. My cousin and I had so much fun that summer, but then came autumn, it was not so warm anymore.

I remember my cousins and I starting kindergarten. One of my cousins was in the same classroom as myself. My mother found out where I was and came up to the school and came to my classroom. The teacher said, "Who are you?" She said, "I came to get my daughter!" The teacher told her she was not on the list. My mother reached inside her pocketbook and pulled out a pair of scissors and told her, "You better get the f—— out of my way before I kill you, b——," and took me and put me in the car with her new husband. His name was Charles Fox.

I remember it was a long ride; it was raining really hard. I fell asleep and I woke up that evening; we were in New York. We were in another Islamic community, there were children my age, we lived in separate houses, the babies were in another house being taken care of by the Muslim women, there were also teenage boys, everybody was separated by age, living in several houses, the Muslim women were separated from the men. I rarely ever saw my mother or my other siblings because my older brother was in another house, and my little sister was in another house, separated by age. My mother had a child on the way who was born in New York. Before we left, my beautiful sister Sadika, my father found out where we were again, so my mother moved back to Philly.

We were back at the community on Fifty-Second and Girard, and we stayed there for a while. My brother and I were not in school. I was seven years old, and my brother was eleven. There we learned how to speak Arabic, spell our names, do exercises, and just play with the other kids.

One day, I was to go to public school on a bus with the rest of the Muslim children. My mother found out and pulled me off the bus. Apparently, she didn't want me to go to school because my father would find out where I was. We were trying to leave the community of Islam that evening. My brother Abdullah stayed behind because he was throwing a big-ass fit. He did not want to go with us. I didn't see him for a long time.

My mother and Charles Fox moved us into this room on Fifty-Second and Baltimore

Avenue in Philadelphia, Pennsylvania. The room was really, really large. It had a hall and an apartment with another Muslim lady and another Muslim brother; they were married. My mother and Charles Fox knew the couple, and they let us come over there to cook our food and use the bathroom.

Soon after a while, we didn't see the couple anymore. They must have moved out. My little sister was abused every day and starved. She barely ate, and they kept her at the other end of the room.

One day, my mother and Charles Fox went out to get some groceries. I'm seven years old, looking at a one-year-old child, Sadika, and my sister Aaliyah. When my mother and Charles Fox returned from the market, I told my mother something that got Aaliyah in trouble. They took Aaliyah into the apartment across the hall. Charles Fox had beaten her. When she came back,

I saw Charles with the stick, and I couldn't even recognize her face; it was so swollen and bloody.

The next day they were to go out again to run some errands. They put us in the apartment across from the room that we were staying in and told us to sit down and watch TV. I didn't know my sister's arm was broken from the night before, and they made her put her arm in this tank of water. When they left, I looked at my sister and told her, "I'm so sorry," and Aaliyah said to me, "It's okay, you did not know." It seems to me that she tried to reassure me that I did not know what was going to happen to her when I told on her.

They beat her so bad that her bottom, she could not sit down, so when she had to eat, she would have to be standing up because her butt was so raw. Most of the time, they would not feed her at all. She would just be lying on the bed on the other side of the room, a very dark room.

One night, on a Friday night, I remember it was Friday because we were watching *The Dukes of Hazzard*. My stepfather Charles Fox went to the other side of the room where Aaliyah was. She had wet the bed, and he picked her up by her neck and slammed her into the wall, and then she fell onto the bed, and all I heard was gurgling noises. My mother went over there and she told us to turn the TV off and recite from the Quran. I guess she was telling us to pray.

My sister lay there for days. I believe she did not die the same night. My sister had flies flying all around her body. The next morning, my mother tried to put a piece of fruit in her mouth. The next day, Charles Fox called a friend, his name was Brother Craig. I remember the trunk was not where it used to be. I did not see Aaliyah's body, but I saw the trunk. My mother told us (me and my sister Sadika) to come on, let's go get something to eat in the next apartment. But I saw Charles Fox and Brother Craig carrying the trunk out of the window. When we went back into the room, nobody was there. My mother told us to sit down and play. She told me if anybody "asks you where Aaliyah is, tell them that she is in New York with her father." My sister Aaliyah was not my father's biological daughter because my mother had an affair with another man, and Aaliyah was still being taken care of by my dad because he forgave my mother. So when he filed for custody, he fought for myself, Abdullah, and Aaliyah, not knowing that Aaliyah was deceased. Remember, my brother Abdullah was not there because he did not come with us.

So I believe, eight months after they threw my sister under the George C. Platt

Memorial Bridge, some PennDOT workers found the trunk and they discovered the brutally battered body of a 4-year-old child. I remember the pain that she endured, and her life was taken away from her at a very, very young age. I don't know why they used to beat her the way they did; she looked so weary – and I'm glad that the Angels came and got her and took her off of this Earth that was so horrible to her.

I used to notice every time my mother was watching TV, she would tell us to go into the other room. I think it must have been on the news when they found her body. Nobody knew who she was, so she was a Jane Doe 28 for almost ten years.

After that, we moved from hotel to hotel every night. Sometimes we would stay with Charles Fox's friends or his mother, and then finally we went to get my brother Abdullah from the Islamic community on

52$^{nd}$ and Girard, and we moved to Richard Allen projects in North Philadelphia. That is the most dangerous and dirtiest part of Philadelphia. My brother Abdullah was with us, but he did not know what happened to baby sister Aaliyah. My brother would ask me every now and then, "Where is Aaliyah?" and I would tell him, "I told you she is in New York with her father."

I told myself that Aaliyah was in New York although I know I saw her put into a trunk, her lifeless body, but I know that was a terrible lie. But my mother made it up because she knew Aaliyah was no longer with us, and at that time, my mother was almost due with another child; her name was Winter.

Now, as for my brother and I, my brother was twelve, and I was nine years old, and Sadika was two. None of us attended school. So, there we were living in the projects, no schooling whatsoever. My brother Abdullah and I would feed my little sister and wash their clothes by hand because we didn't have a washing machine. I had to bathe them, feed them, of course, clean the house, meaning, all of the chores.

If we did something that my mother didn't like, she would tell Charles Fox when he came in from whatever he was doing, working outside, I guess, and we were getting beaten with whatever he could find, beating until we were bloody the same way that used to beat Aaliyah and worse, with a stick or two by four. On one occasion, my mother was mad at Abdullah for something very small and threw a hot pot of water in his face, and he had boils all over his face, and he had puffy black eyes and could not open them.

When she used to beat us and choke us, we would have scratches all over our necks. Another punishment, my mother will tell me and Abdullah not to eat anything for about a week, but sometimes she would tell me after three days to go ahead and eat and leave Abdullah to starve. We still had to cook and feed the little ones. After we were done feeding the children, she would call us upstairs.

My mother would ask us, "Did y'all eat?" and we would say no. Then she would say, "Well, let me smell your breath." One day she called me into the room after three days of not eating. She would tell me that I could go ahead and eat and let my brother starve for another two days. So after the punishment, everything was the same, getting beatings and choked. Other times, I don't remember what I did, my mother tied my hands behind my back, told my brother Abdullah to tie some other belts together, at least four or five of them, told him to tie them together, and she threw me on the bed and beat me with the belts. I was in so much pain. Charles Fox wasn't there during the daytime. He used to be a vendor, selling clothes, earrings, incense, bracelets, belts, and finger rings. My brother Abdullah and I used to stay up while everyone else was asleep, putting the incense and oil in bags, polishing earrings, and arranging them on boards for him to sell.

We also had to make the brass bracelets. We had to put them under a torch, shave them on the ends, put designs on them, and make sure they were bendable so they could roll around your arms. We had to arrange the finger rings in cases for display. So we used to take care of the children, wash clothes by hand in the tub, cook dinner, and all of the other meals—all while being on punishment and getting starved.

We also had to fast during Ramadan, a Muslim tradition. We made five prayers a day. Though there was no school, my mother did buy us a lot of books, so we were literate. We learned math and read the Quran as well.

Now, I remember that Charles Fox would be in the bathroom for God knows how long. Come to find out later, when in years my brother met one of the Muslim brothers that used to live on Fifty-Second and Girard at the Nation of Islam, come to find out that Charles Fox was on heroin. Of course, later on in the years, we would ask our mother, and she would say she didn't know anything about it.

I remember Charles Fox would wake me up in the middle of the night and tell me to make him a cake or his other favorite, banana pudding—you know, the kind that you have to make on the stove. I used to be so mad that I wanted to cry.

So we only stayed living at Richard Allen projects from 1982 to 1984. We moved from there because my father found where we were living once again and we had to move. He finally got supervised visits. Meanwhile, my mother was still collecting welfare checks for my deceased sister, Aaliyah Davis.

So after a while, we moved to what appeared to be an abandoned house in West Philadelphia on Paulson Avenue. There wasn't a porch, so we had to put crates there to climb up into the house. In the winter, the house was freezing cold, and the toilet didn't flush, so we didn't have running water. There was a broken pipe in the basement that water came out of, which my older brother would fill up every day, at least fifty buckets of water to pour down the toilet after we used it.

My mother and Charles Fox made Abdullah clean the toilet and dip out all of the feces and put that in the basement. At this time, my mother called it home. There were three bedrooms. My mother and Charles Fox slept in the back room. Next to the bathroom, there was another room where we kept all the food—cans and boxes of food. After that, it was the bathroom, and then there was a small room where my brother Abdullah slept. Next to that was the front room where I and the girls slept. So now it was me, my sister Sadika, and the baby that was born, Winter. Her name was Winter. My mother would give birth to another baby girl in a couple of months. There was no heat in the house, so we had to cook food on a kerosene heater and stuff like that, making grilled cheese on the light bulb.

One winter in 1985, it was very, very freezing cold. My mother and Charles Fox had to get an extra heater and they put it in the room with me and the girls, and another mattress for them to sleep on. They did not give Abdullah any heat to heat his room where he slept. That winter, in December 1986, a baby girl was born. Shy Shy was her name.

She was very beautiful and very peaceful; she did not cry, all she did was look around.

She was born in the back room of the abandoned house that we lived in. A midwife delivered her in the back room. As Mommy dearest held the newborn baby girl, she healed from having the newborn baby and went back to her same evil ways. One day, she went out to do some errands, and she told me to give the kids some fruit when they woke up.

So when I tried to get the children the fruit, they said they didn't want that, so I tried to give them cereal. When my mother came back, she asked the kids what did they eat, and they said cereal. My mother came and choked me and got a knife and stabbed me in my arms because I gave them cereal. I fell and hit my head on the corner of a table that had a small black and white TV on it. I was knocked unconscious. When I came through, I saw my mother standing over top of me, yelling and shouting at me to get up, and she looked very scared.

The look on her face showed that she probably thought she'd kill another one of her children. But I got up and I shook it off. She screamed at me, telling me to clean the f—— up.

On another occasion, my brother Abdullah and I were to eat some salmon for lunch. We thought that the salmon didn't taste right, so we threw it in the trash. When my mother found out, she told us to bring up the trash can and made us eat it out of the trash can.

Of course, we got sick, but she didn't care at all. On another occasion, she made my brother Abdullah and me drink a bottle of castor oil. Even sitting here talking about it, I think of the smell and the taste. After a while, it makes me sick, literally.

The baby girl that was born in December is walking now. Soon, around the time we moved into this big house on Fifty-First and Springfield Avenue in Philadelphia, Pennsylvania. This was the best living situation we were ever in.

The way it was set up was the girls were on the top floor, the third floor. My mother was in the front room on the third floor, and my three little sisters were in the bedroom on the third floor. The youngest baby girl stayed in the front room with my mother, now pregnant with another baby.

Now on the second floor, my brother Abdullah stayed in the back room. Next to the bathroom, was next to the steps that led down to the kitchen. Down the hall was a room in the front. On the second floor was where Charles Fox slept. Stairs next to his room led down to the living room to the front door.

Most of the time, my brother Abdullah, my baby sisters, and I would stay downstairs, cooking, cleaning, and making sure the children's hair was done and they had clean clothes on.

Of course, we were still not in school and couldn't play outside with the neighborhood children. Yes, we're teenagers now. I was thirteen and Abdullah was sixteen years old. My mother stayed upstairs on the third floor always, never really coming downstairs except to go out of the door.

So you know how teenagers are and what we could get into. So we started sneaking out and meeting people. I had this one girl, her name was Sandy. I used to sneak out and go over to her house while my mother was not there. My brother Abdullah liked the girl Sandy that we used to sneak into the house.

Of course, my mother didn't know because she was all the way up on the third floor. We needed somebody to stand guard, so I would stay and check on the steps coming down to the living room, and Abdul would watch the steps coming through the kitchen. I had a big crush on the guy who used to visit my brother, but he was sixteen and I was like thirteen. My brother Abdul liked my girlfriend Sandy. We started getting really bold, sneaking them into the house because remember, my mother used to never come downstairs, so we could let them in through the back gate.

One time, we almost got caught because it snowed that day and our friend came to the gate and whistled. My brother tried to hurry to go to the window to warn him away because Charles Fox was in the bathroom, and that was right next to Abdul's room that led to the back gate. Charles Fox came into the room and asked my brother what that noise was. My brother said he did not know, so Charles Fox took one of my brother's shoes and went outside because he saw footprints and tried to compare the boot print.

Then he came back up the steps and choked and punched my brother, asking why he was outside because that was his footprint. He screamed at my brother, "Why the f*** were you outside?" We all heard the noise from the third floor that was coming from the second floor. All we heard was him beating my brother for about ten minutes.

The next day, Charles and my mother went out to do errands. My brother Abdul snuck into Charles Fox's room, and that's when we discovered the music group New Edition. We found teenage magazines in there like *Black Beat* magazine that had all the posters of superstars. So every time they went out (my mother and Fox), we used to take the New Edition album and record them onto a cassette tape.

I took the teen magazines and the pictures of New Edition's singer out of the book and hung them on my wall. That was very bold, right? But we didn't want him to know we snuck in his room. But with the pictures up, I don't know what I was thinking. I guess I was just so in love with New Edition and the lead singer was my favorite. I always posted on my wall, the nerve.

Then I picked a pen pal out of the magazine; he lived in New Mexico. So funny, we got really bold and found a puzzle book that had code letters in it. We memorized the code letters like they were regular alphabets to sneak secret notes. So if it was found, they wouldn't be able to read the note.

It's funny now to me; it wasn't back then. We were playing a dangerous game. My mother got mad one day and tore all my New Edition posters off of my walls. Charles Fox found out that Abdullah had a pen pal. I just said he figured that we were sneaking into his room. He just went into my brother's room and started throwing things around as if he were looking for something.

That's when he found one of our secret notes and a letter from Abdul's pen pal. It's so crazy, the secret note that he found, the letter was releasing how we were going to poison him because we wanted to kill him for abusing us. And I know I wanted him dead for killing my sister Aaliyah, which Abdullah knew nothing about. I'm pretty sure he knew because he remembers when my mother killed Saaid.

We're getting older and sick and tired of the abuse. Just sitting thinking about all of this, the evil things that happened to us, like the time my mother got mad at me because the oven was making the house too hot when she was the one that told me to cook dinner. She told me to come up the steps.

When I got up the steps, she kicked me in my face, and I fell down all of those steps that lead from the upstairs straight to the kitchen. There was no landing or anything, just straight down. I could have really fallen and broken my neck. But did she give a s——? No another time my mother was in one of her rages and took it out on Aaliyah. She put his head through a glass window and broke the glass with his head and his face.

I remember one day it was February 28, which was Aaliyah's birthday. My mother came down in the kitchen and sat down. She said, "Do y'all want to bake a cake for Aaliyah's birthday?" My brother and I got quiet and just looked at each other silently. Remember, I was there when Aaliyah was murdered, not Abdul. I know that my brother Abdullah knew that Aaliyah was gone just like our brother Saaid, no longer with us physically, just angels watching over us. He still would ask me about her; sometimes I wouldn't answer him, and sometimes I just told him that she was in New York with her father. I believe that she really was in New York because that's where I wanted to be, although I saw her dead body being carried out of the window inside of a steam trunk.

So my mother is pregnant with another baby by Charles Fox, too, my baby brother would be their fourth child together. I know I had nightmares every night since that happened, and she would come to me in my dreams, and I was so scared when I woke up. So my mother has a midwife; her name was Iris. She looked like some type of hippie, lol. She's the lady who delivered my mother's third baby girl by Charles.

One morning at the crack of dawn, my mother woke me up out of my sleep because she was having contractions. As soon as she woke me up, I heard a loud gush that sounded like a bunch of water; the baby was about to be born. So we didn't have a phone to call the midwife; stupid ass Charles Fox went to the pay phone and called the hippy midwife. So there was no stopping what was a good surprise baby boy; the baby was coming fast. My mother laid down on the bed and called me to come over to her. She told me to hold my hands out not to let the baby fall; it was coming, and out of nowhere, I helped pull the baby out. He came head first; he took his first breath, and I didn't even have to spank him, like the doctors do. I got a nice clean towel to clean him off, and then here comes Charles Fox stumbling up the steps with his goofy ass, and the midwife Iris a day late and a dollar short. The only thing she did was cut the cord because I already pulled him out and cleaned him off with the washcloth and the clean towels; thank God that the cord wasn't wrapped around his Little Neck. All of the major stuff I did; the midwife was delivering babies for $500, so she came after everything was done. So with all that being said, I feel like somebody owes me $500 with interest, lol.

So it's been a couple of years since the last time we saw our father. That was when he was trying to get visitation from us, Mr. Davis, my father won the right to give unsupervised visits at his home for me and Abdullah and Aaliyah; but of course Aaliyah could not come because she was gone, going from this earth. I believe that's why we moved out of that abandoned house to Fifty-First and Springfield, but of course, they found out where she was because she was on welfare. I don't know what she thought running from house to house. So the house that we were in now, my father was awarded unsupervised visits, and he picked us up from that house, and we started going to his house. My mother told us not to talk to him and not to eat anything over there because he probably would put something in our food, and that he eats pork. My mother was extra salty; she didn't want us, Abdullah and I, with my dad alone because I knew she feared that it would be found out about Aaliyah being dead. So she told people that my father was on drugs and that he had molested me, which I knew wasn't true—a horrible, horrible lie made up by this baby killer, a serial killer because if you kill more than one person, that makes you a serial killer from what I understand. So that's what she told us to brainwash us. I was much too smart for that, and so was my brother. When we started going over to the house, this is me and my dad and my brother; we would just sit there and didn't say anything to my dad the whole visit. My mother told us that he is a jinn (the devil in Arabic). So the first couple of visits we did not speak to our father, and we did not do anything because my mother never told us not to, believing that my dad would try to poison us. When he tried to start conversations with us, we didn't at all.

On about the third visit, my brother started talking and having conversations, something my mother told us not to do. Then we started eating and having a good time. My dad even took us to the store to buy us clothes because we were always dressed up as Muslims.

On about the fourth visit, we started changing our clothes and going to lunch, movies, and dinner, and things like that. My father bought me my first Bobby Brown cassette tape; I was overjoyed. We were having so much fun getting to know our father and reuniting with family from Baltimore.

On one visit, which was the last time we saw our little sisters and newborn baby brother when it came time to end the visit, we were supposed to be back at my mother's house at eight o'clock. When the visit ended at eight o'clock, my older brother Abdullah looked at my dad and said, "I'm not going back." We did not return to Mommy Dearest's house that evening.

So it was summer 1987, we were not locked up in the house, and then we were not beaten and choked and getting our heads thrown through windows, and hot water boiling water thrown in our faces. We were able to play with the neighborhood kids. Of course, we had chores, dishes, cleaning our rooms, and things of the sort. We already knew how to cook, and we loved to cook, and big things I can do for our little sisters.

Everything that we experienced, the abuse we endured, was in our past, a breath of fresh air. The summer was coming to an end. I stayed down in Baltimore, Maryland, most of all the summer, went to Dorney Park and Six Flags Great Adventure, and went to the beach. Soon I came back to Philadelphia. It was going into autumn; the weather was getting cooler.

My father took me and my older brother shopping for school. We were no longer dressed up like Muslims. We went to school grade-appropriate. I was in the eighth grade, and my brother was in the ninth grade. I was fourteen; he was sixteen.

As time went on, I started doing crazy things like running away because my father would not let me talk to my boyfriend on the phone.

My dad wouldn't let me see my boyfriend, so I ran away. I went around the corner from where my mother was staying, the house on Fifty-First and Springfield. My father found out where I was and chased me, putting me in the van that he was driving. He took me back home and sent me to my room. I started screaming and crying. He came back upstairs and asked me why I was screaming and hollering, and I started screaming my sister Aaliyah's name.

He said, "Aaliyah? What about Aaliyah?" Now remember, I was the only one who knew what happened to her because my other sister was only one year old and in her crib, and I was seven, just turned eight, because Abdul wasn't there when this occurred with Aaliyah being tortured and starved and she passed away. I told my father that Aaliyah was dead. Everyone in the house was crying.

The next morning, my father called my uncle, who knew someone who worked at The Roundhouse in the homicide department. They took me down there and asked me some questions. They took me to the rooftop of the Roundhouse; the detective showed me the trunk that Aaliyah was thrown in, and I told him the trunk that Leah was in was black.

He told me that it was black but had faded from being in the sun for so many years. I was crying.

Then they took me into an interview room and asked me what had happened. I told them what happened, but it was a Friday night, and Aaliyah was beaten to death. Although I don't think she died that night, that's what led to her death, and she didn't because I remember my mother trying to put food in her mouth instead of calling for help. She would rather let my sister sit there in all that pain and die like that instead of taking her to the hospital. She was worried about getting locked up.

Aaliyah was kept alone on the other side of this very large room. Charles Fox went on the side of the room where Aaliyah laid in the bed, laying there sick and weak with broken arms and broken ribs. Aaliyah wet the bed, and he picked her up by her neck and threw her against the wall. Then he choked her, and she fell on the bed gasping for air.

Aaliyah didn't die that night; a few days later, I believe she did because my mother kept trying to put food in her mouth. The flies were around her body until Charles Fox had one Muslim brother, who they called Brother Craig, put her lifeless body into the trunk and sheets. They threw her under the George C. Platt Memorial Bridge in Philadelphia, Pennsylvania. Many years went by; she was a nameless Jane Doe before the FBI put out arrests for Charles and my mother. They fled, avoiding capture.

Meanwhile, my brother Abdul and I went away to a group home named Carson Valley for children with behavioral issues. This would be the first time that I would be in a school with children my age and older, of course, besides kindergarten. But all my brother went to was first grade, and that was it. I was so happy. Everything, but everything, was not as I thought it was. I thought and was taught that if you treat people nicely, they will treat you nicely as well.

They used to tease me and try to start fights with me. I did not react to them, so they kept messing with me until I punched this one girl in her face, and we fought. Of course, nobody messed with me after that.

My brother Abdul got into his first fight the second day that we were there, and I ran away with a couple of boys and girls from the cottage where we stayed. The cottage I stayed in was coed, meaning there were girls on one side of the building and boys on the other side. That night, it was freezing cold, and some of us ran away, but we soon returned. We were all sorry and were placed on restriction for three days. Three days of sitting on the bench and not going to the rec center to play ball or just to socialize, jump rope, and things like that

that children my age did. Or I was refused a home pass, which I really didn't care about because I didn't go home on all of my home passes. I'd rather have stayed with the children at the school. This was a cottage called Lower Beach, or short-term, meaning that a person would only be there for three to six months.

So when my review came up, it was decided that I was to go to long-term college, the college up the road called Upper Beach. I moved up there. The girls were much older and well-behaved and didn't start fights like the younger children on short terms. My brother Abdullah was up for review, and he was sent to a long-term college called Storek Hill. Long-term meant you stay there until you graduate, and they would show you how to live independently, find you an apartment, and make sure you had work. After that, you were thrown to the wolves, if you will. LOL. The world will not welcome you with open arms.

So I had to go to school on grounds because my behavior was not as well as could be accepted to go to the high school off grounds (Springfield High School), but my grades were good enough to run track. So I went to school on grounds during the daytime. After lunch I went to a trade school for hair, Vo-Tech for cosmetology, and then I ran track. After that, I came home and did homework, ate dinner, and went to the Rec at night. I even made the honor roll. I was very busy and stayed focused. My older brother Abdullah and I went to therapy two to three times a week. It was really crazy how when we went to therapy, the therapist would just sit there and look at us for a whole hour and didn't say anything.

So my mother was on America's Most Wanted for violating probation, the murder of my brother and my baby sister, collecting welfare for my deceased sister's abusive corpse, and not having us in school, among numerous other charges. We were fourteen and sixteen with no schooling up until now. My brother, my father, and I were on America's Most Wanted telling the story about my mother so she could be captured by authorities. The FBI really needed to capture her right away because they had my other three sisters and the baby boy with them. It was really frightening at the thought that my siblings were with them. I was really scared that Charles Fox would kill another one of my siblings and my mother as well. I knew what they were capable of because I lived and saw it for myself, and my older brother Abdullah also knew about the murder of the other baby boy who was killed at two years old. Two weeks after America's Most Wanted, the FBI caught my mother and Charles Fox in Virginia. One morning, I was getting dressed, and one of the staff members at

Carson Valley came into my room and told me that I had a phone call. When I picked up the phone, it was my father. He called to inform me that my mother and Charles Fox had been caught in Virginia.

My heart dropped into my stomach. Everybody sounded and acted very happy, but I was having mixed feelings because she was my mother. But I knew what she was capable of. For some reason, I was sad and angry at the same time. She needed to be in jail for what she had done. I believe after killing more than one person, you become a serial killer. She was a serial child abuser and murderer. So I knew she needed to be incarcerated and have the book thrown at her, period—to be in jail before they could kill another one. It could have been any one of the children she had with her. A couple of months, Abdullah decided we did not want to return to my mother's. It was told to me that my mother started abusing the younger siblings after Abdullah and I left. The way my mother and Charles Fox used to abuse us, they started abusing the oldest of Charles Fox's kids, Sadika. I really felt that it was going to be her if another one was killed. She told me a lot of stories about what happened to her after we left while they were in Virginia.

So it was 1988, and the trial began for my mother and Charles Fox. I think that's when my behavior began to turn for the worst. My mother was a baby serial killer. I still love my mother and need her, even today. I question my own sanity for still dealing with her. But at the same time, I feel that I cannot hold hate in my heart because, as I tell people who ask me why I deal with her, she has to answer to God for that, and it's not for me to judge her. And that makes any sense.

Soon a couple of months passed, and then the trial started. I didn't know the day before or anything because the staff didn't tell me, I guess they thought that I might have gone away. So the trial went on for a couple of weeks. I believe that's when my behavior took a turn for the worse. Before that, I was a model citizen. The trial went on for a week, which seemed like forever. It seemed my mom's side of the family turned on my big brother Abdullah and me. They were saying that we were lying about my mother. I don't see what the hell could have been made up. I mean, there were two dead children. What could I have been lying about?

So my maternal grandmother was taking care of my mother's children, my siblings, when my grandmother seemed like she didn't want to have anything to do with me and Abdul, like we were the black sheep of the family, when here she had her daughter kill two of her kids. But we were frowned upon.

The trial was very hard. Seeing my mother and Charles Fox. I don't know why, but I was still scared. Scared of my mother and that evil man. All of the evil things they used to do to us, myself and my siblings. I was very afraid for my little sisters when my mother and Charles Fox fled to Virginia, avoiding authorities. But I want my sister, the oldest out of the youngest, to tell her story when they were in Virginia because I was not there. The abuse was really bad for her, as well as it used to be for us, my brother Abdul and I. It was a very scary time for her, and only she herself will tell you that.

My mother got sentenced to fifteen years, and Charles Fox to fifteen to thirty-five years. My mother only did fourteen years in prison, getting out in 2001. Charles Fox got out in 2022. Bittersweet, I don't know, but I guess I was expecting an apology, but I have not gotten one, none of us. My brother

Abdul and the rest of the children, most of them like the last two of her kids, did not know about it or the pain that we endured.

I was so hurt that my mother was going to jail because I was becoming a teenager, and I needed my mother. But I guess I did not really like getting beaten the hell out of me every day, and neither did the rest of us. My grandmother set up visits for my siblings to come up to the school to visit my brother Abdullah and me twice a month. I was always so happy to see them. We were able to take the children off the grounds to the restaurant for ice cream. Although my older brother and I didn't bring up what had happened, the pain was still there, and we were all so lost, especially the younger ones. When my grandmother came to pick the kids up on one visit, I asked her for her address.

After the trial was over, it seemed like I didn't care about much anymore. I had run away and went to my grandmother's house. I stayed there for a couple of days, then I really started seeing that she did not want me there because she thought I had lied, so she brought me back up to the school. After that, every weekend, I would just leave and go to the movies with my boyfriend, stuff like that, Dorney Park. I was just doing what I wanted to do. I would start fights with people in the school, just doing whatever I wanted to do, stuff that I didn't have to do. I was in so much pain.

So usually, if a kid is supposed to be kicked out of the school, they would give you a thirty-day notice. This time, they didn't give me a thirty-day notice, they gave me a day's notice. So my father did not want me to come home to live with him, I guess because I had bad behavior problems, so I went to live with my great-grandmother in North Philadelphia. I did not like living there; it was depressing. I did not really know her well, but I found that she was mean to me, as well as the rest of everybody. This one aunt on my mother's side is the only one that did not turn her back on me. She let me come stay with her when I had nowhere to go. Then I stayed with her, and then I met my daughter's father.

My daughter is thirty years old right now, but I went to live with my daughter's father and his mother for a while. And then I left, and I went to live back with my aunt, the one who let me stay with her when I didn't have anywhere to go. So I met my son's father. I got pregnant, and when I was eighteen, I had my first baby boy. I had to sell drugs so that I could feed myself. Soon after I had the baby, I met my daughter's father again because we had broken up. As soon as I had my son, I got pregnant with my daughter. My first two were eleven months apart, so then I had my daughter eleven months later. I didn't even wait; eleven months after that,

I had my third child. I had three children eleven months apart. Soon after that, I was very unstable and didn't have a place for me and my children to live, so I went to shelters. My first son's grandmother even let me stay with her and her family for a while. I met my godmother; she let me stay with her, and even when people talked about me behind my back, she wouldn't hear of it. She would say, "Don't talk about my godchild. I'm sitting right here." She knew I had a lot going on and a lot of pain in my life.

So soon after, years went by, and I wound up on drugs and drinking, and then, for a while, I pulled myself together. I started working, and that's when I got pregnant with my fourth child. I was working for a couple of years and wasn't drinking and doing drugs, but after my fourth child, me and his dad broke up, and I went back to drugs and drinking because I was really so hurt. Before it was all over, I had six kids, and I never really was stable until I met my last son's father. He was an older man; this was in 1998 when I met him. When I was pregnant with my fifth child, I rented a room from him while I was working. Then I had the baby. Not too long after he was born, me and my son's father, the one that is the youngest, developed a relationship. He took care of me; he only wanted the best for me. But he was sixty-five, and then he passed away from cancer. So after I had the baby by him, he died two weeks after my son turned one. I was very hurt, and then I turned back to drinking and drugs. Of course, I got evicted from the house because I was not taking care of things; I just totally lost it. I even tried to commit suicide. I went to live in shelters, and then I finally went to this place called Family House. It was like a rehab where a mother could take her children, but only the children under fourteen, so I wound up living at the Family House. I did not complete the program; I only stayed there for four months, and then I left and got a little apartment. Then, a couple of months later, that's when I met my husband, and he saved my life. Now I am clean of drugs and alcohol, and I feel so wonderful. Although I have issues with my health because I slipped and fell and hit my head like three years ago, so now I have memory loss, and I'm always sleepy and tired. And I'm glad that I'm off of drugs because I'm able to see and take care of my grandkids and not be drunk and belligerent around them.

I really regret the way things were. I did not raise most of my children because I was always unsettled with my living situation. But now, all of my children are grown up, and they know, and most of them forgive me because they saw what I went through. I guess they understand why, and they are very forgiving, and I love that about my children. Most of them, anyway, understand.

It's like we were on a mission. I believe it was the summer of 1989, and I was in a lot of pain after my mother's and stepfather's trials. My mother was sentenced to fourteen years in a Pennsylvania prison in Muncie, Pennsylvania. I was so sad, hurt, and heartbroken. I missed my little sisters, whom my mother and her new husband brought into the world together. My mother married my stepfather in New York while she was still legally married to my father, Charles Fox. My mother murdered my five-year-old sister while she was still on probation for murdering my older brother before I was born—he was only two years old.

Wow, six years' probation for killing a little boy. But he was only a little Black boy, so I guess it didn't matter much. Anyway, the system allowed her to have her remaining children back in her custody as soon as she was released. I can't help but think that if my

mother had been given jail time for murdering
my older brother, she wouldn't have been able
to murder my baby sister Aaliyah. That's the
sad part. To this day, they are taking children
away from their mothers for foolish reasons,
when there are much more severe cases—like
kids being starved, locked in cages, brutally
beaten, or murdered by their mothers, fathers,
or adoptive parents.

After my mother was sentenced to prison,
I caused so much trouble and confusion at
the group home where I lived—starting
fights with the residents and staff, getting
kicked out of class every day, and just being
a menace. I was only given a day's notice
to be off the grounds, probably by the next
afternoon. I really needed professional help,
but I guess no one was equipped or educated
enough to handle a person with my mental
state or behavior. Months before I was kicked
out of Carson Valley School, I was sent to an

institution because I tried to commit suicide. I had to stay there for thirty days before being returned to Carson Valley. I was okay for a while.

After I was given that day's notice to leave Carson Valley, I didn't return to my father's house but went to my great-grandmother's house in North Philadelphia—the same people who turned their backs on my brother Abdul and me, saying that we lied about my mother. We had to testify about the abuse and other things. I stayed with my great-grandmother until I was shipped off to West Virginia to Job Corps, a school where you learn a trade. Of course, things didn't work out at my great-grandmother's. It was really sad and depressing being there, so I went to this place called Youth Emergency Service and waited for my name to be called to go to Job Corps.

While I was at the Youth Emergency shelter, we were allowed to go out but had to be back by curfew: 11:00 p.m. on weekends and 9:00 p.m. during the week. This place was located in Center City, Philadelphia. At 16 you could get into a lot of trouble not being supervised. It was so crazy at this place.

I was having what you would call an affair with one of the staff members—his name was Eli. One of the girls I hung out with was also messing around with one of the staff members. They used to take us shopping and do things like that. These men were in their thirties.

At night, I would sneak downstairs while everyone was asleep to go see Eli, who was supposed to be making sure we were safe in the building. On the weekends, some of us would go to Penn's Landing, chill, sit by the boats, and look at the water. As time went on, we got bored and started getting into mischief. I was always the ringleader, telling the girls what to do.

It started off with us snatching people's bags as they came out of the Gallery—the mall in Center City—grabbing bags and earrings. Some nights, I remember telling one of the girls to smack another girl who was standing at the bus stop, smoking a cigarette. I told her to snatch the cigarette out of her mouth too, and we all thought it was funny. It really wasn't, of course, and I know that now since I'm older. It was like we were on a mission, just doing stupid stuff to pass the time, hurting innocent people. I hope God forgives me for that ignorant moment in my life.

It's the staff used to take us on trip, one of the trips we would go on was the pool at passyunk in South Philadelphia, and that's where I met the man who would become my daughter's father years down the line. What a summer that was.

The summer came and went without warning, and I got the call that I was supposed to leave for Job Corps the next day. My heart sank because I had met someone I thought I loved. When I got the call, I didn't want to leave, so I called the guy I had met, and he came to get me. That evening, we met at Fifteenth and Market Street in Center City, Philadelphia, and I stayed over at his friend's house in Passyunk Projects with him.

There, I didn't do much. Most of the time, there wasn't any food for me to eat. We'd grab something from the mini-market and run out without paying, then head to the pool. As the weather got chilly, I didn't have anywhere to live or anything to eat. My mother was in jail, and I couldn't live with her or my father because I was supposed to go to Job Corps. I remembered that my aunt had told me where she lived—on York Street in North Philadelphia—so I found her.

My aunt welcomed me and my boyfriend with open arms. I remember her from my childhood; she was my brother Abdul's and my favorite aunt. I stayed with her for a while, but my boyfriend and I didn't stay together long. I was very hurt because life and people weren't what I thought they were. I had been sheltered from the world and had a different perspective on life. I was in for a rude awakening.

I was raised Muslim, and I believed that when a man and a woman loved each other and had children, the man was supposed to take care of the house. But I guess that wasn't true in real life. I suppose I had been living in a fantasy world.

I was living with my beautiful aunt, who kept me from being homeless, along with her husband, my favorite Uncle Al. One day, my uncle got off work early, and I was sitting on the steps outside, feeling very depressed. My uncle's sister came out of the house, and she asked me, "Girl, what's wrong with you?"

I looked up at her, knowing she had kids my age, and I asked, "Can I come with you?" She looked at me like she felt my pain, like she knew I was depressed, and replied, "Come on, girl." That made me feel better. This lady didn't know anything about me, just that my aunt was married to her brother, a beautiful woman indeed for her and her husband to take me and just like that.

I have had many blessings, and they were one of them. I stayed with them for a while. We didn't live in the best conditions, but they would not see me on the street. All the weekends, we would go across the street to my fairy godmother's girlfriend's house, and we used to drink. I got so drunk one night that I fell asleep, and when I woke up, this man was on top of me, having sex with me—a very much older guy than I was. I was only seventeen, and he was like fiftysomething.

After a while, I met my fairy godmother's nephew, and we started talking. I was so hungry at times that I had to sell drugs to get money for food—a very dangerous thing to do. My boyfriend, my fairy godmother's nephew, for women and I started dealing drugs and that way I had money for food. He, another family member of his, and I would take shifts selling cocaine.

On one occasion, the guy we were selling for came to count the money and gave us more drugs to sell. When we ran out, after my shift, he counted my money and drugs, and the count didn't come out right. I was tired the night before, and my so-called boyfriend had stolen my share of the money or drugs because he did my shift for me. This could have gotten me killed, but the guy just told me to go ahead and work it off, so I did.

We were selling in North Philadelphia near Broad Street and Allegheny, operating out of an abandoned building. We work inside of a lock room in an abandoned house. One day, early in the daytime, someone knocked on the door. Thinking it was someone who wanted to buy drugs, I went to answer it. As I did, I heard someone say, "We about to stick these b—— ass n—— up." I quickly told my boyfriend and his other family members. We dropped everything and ran out the back door. As we ran, we saw who it was—they were actually related to my boyfriend by marriage somehow. We kept running all the way to my aunt's house on York Street.

After that, we ended up staying with my aunt again. Soon, I found out I was pregnant with my first son. I realized it because I kept getting nauseous, and my godmother kept telling me I was pregnant. I was really depressed. One night, I was just walking around crying when a man in a car pulled up beside me. He stopped and asked if I was okay. Seeing that I was crying, he asked why I was out there. "What, you don't have anywhere to go?" he asked.

I looked at him, not feeling like I was in any danger, and said, "No, I don't have anywhere to go." He pulled over and told me to get in, so I did. This man, whom I didn't know, took me to some old lady's house, where they had a conversation. The woman then told me to come inside. She took me upstairs, gave me a towel, and let me clean myself up. She also gave me a nightgown to sleep in. That night, I was in a nice, clean bed and felt safe. I went to sleep.

The next day, I slept until the afternoon. She didn't even wake me or bother me. When I finally woke up, I went to the bathroom and washed my jeans, shirt, and underwear by hand. She came to check on me and asked if I needed anything. I just asked if she had a dryer so I could dry my clothes, and she said yes. She told me to come downstairs and made me something to eat. After I finished eating, she gave me my dry clothes. I don't even remember us having much of a conversation.

I got myself dressed and groomed, bid the nice lady farewell, and thanked her so much. She said, "You're welcome, sweetheart," and then I left. It was a nice day outside, so I walked over to my aunt's house. We all sat on the steps, just talking like it was another day in the hood. Meanwhile, every day I became more certain that I was going to have a baby. Secretly, I was thinking that I couldn't just sit there and do nothing to improve my situation for myself and my child.

God is so good all the time. What I mean by that is how He placed that lady, who let me rest in her house, in my life—even for that moment—when I needed an angel. With that being said, I knew I couldn't just sit there, pregnant, without trying to make a better plan for my child, my little bambino. One morning, I woke up and decided to walk to the lady's house. I'll call her Angel. I walked over to Angel's house, and she let me in without hesitation.

I asked her, "Can I see your Yellow Pages?"

She said, "Sure," and I told her I just needed to use her phone. I was looking for a shelter where I could go to get housing for me and my baby.

I made a couple of phone calls and found a shelter. They told me they had one spot and that I needed to be there by five o'clock. I was sick that morning, dealing with morning sickness, and I hadn't eaten or drunk anything. I didn't even have bus fare. But I had a gift from God—my beautiful feet and legs—and I walked from North Philadelphia to Fifty-Sixth and Haverford. I didn't tell anybody where I was going. I was pregnant with my first son and didn't know what the hell I was going to do.

While I was at the shelter, I met a girl named Sabrina. We used to hang out and play around. The shelter had a pay phone that the residents could use to make calls. One day, Sabrina was on the phone, and I walked by and said, "You sound happy! Who are you talking to?"

She replied, "I'm talking to some guy named Rob that I met."

I said, "Oh yeah? Where's he from?"

She said, "Passyunk Projects."

I said, "Oh s——! Do you know someone named Malik?"

She said yes.

I said, "Wow!" So Rob went and got Malik, and I started talking to him again. We stayed on the phone until 3:00 a.m. when I ran out of quarters. The next day, we made plans to see each other. Malik and Rob came to see me and my homegirl Sabrina.

Eventually, I left the shelter and stayed with Malik, his mother, and his sisters. Six months later, I started going back over to my aunt's house on York Street. One day, I got bored, so I walked over to Malik's house, but he wasn't there. There was another girl there, though, and she was pregnant, waiting for Malik too. I believed I had seen her before when I went to South Philly or Passyunk Projects, but I hadn't paid her any mind. She saw me as well, and that was that—until we saw each other again this time around.

Of course, Malik's sister, who loved making trouble, introduced the girl and me. She loved to stir up confusion because she had nothing else to do. She knew where Malik was and walked both of us—me and the pregnant girl—to where he was. His sister confronted her brother right in front of us. I don't know why she thought it was any of her business. Malik, standing there in front of us, looked really high and had a dumb look on his face. His sister got a kick out of it, so we started asking him questions. We all started walking together, and he was backed into a corner.

Now that the girl and I knew who each other was, I knew her as Malik's girlfriend and the mother of his baby. I was very deeply hurt although I was pregnant with someone else's child because Malik and I hadn't seen each other for a while before we met again after I was pregnant And myself and his child's mother all talked that's why he was playing both of us. He was really backed into a corner and had to decide who he was going to choose—me or his child's mother. He decided then and there to choose his child's mother.

Later that night, he walked her to the train station. She lived in Delaware, which was a long way from his mother's place on Sixteenth and Allegheny in North Philadelphia. When he came back from walking her to the train, he asked me, "Can we talk?"

I said, "What could you possibly want to talk about? You made your decision."

Still, I let him talk. He told me, "I love you and want to be with you, but I only told my girlfriend that I wanted to be with her because she's pregnant with my child. If I break it off with her, she'll abort the baby."

Pregnant and emotional, I settled for what he said—silly me. I accepted it and went along with being his girlfriend…his *other* girlfriend. It was weird because I was raised in the Islamic faith, and it wasn't strange for me to accept that a man could have more than one wife. But Islam also says a man can have more than one wife only if he can afford to take care of them. Lord knows that wasn't true in this case—Malik didn't have a pot to piss in or a window to throw it out of. He was living with his mother and didn't even have a job. His mother was battling a drug addiction, and neither of his sisters was in school. He grew up without a father and apparently knew nothing about being a real man.

It was really hard being seventeen, living on the streets, and moving from house to house. My aunt never turned me away when I needed to stay with her and her husband in their small efficiency apartment.

Between my boyfriend Malik's mother and my aunt, they really helped me out. I couldn't have been on the street with nowhere to go. Being so young and on the street by myself, hungry again, I turned to selling drugs to support myself. I often think about how many people I hurt by selling poison to them. I sold crack cocaine to many people around me.

The last couple of months of my pregnancy, I stayed on Sixteenth and Allegheny with Malik. I visited my aunt on the weekends while living on Sixtieth and Allegheny. I had my first son on the way. In the middle of the night, I felt like I had to go to the bathroom, and I woke Malik up out of his sleep and told him how I felt. And he yelled out Mommy amira's water broke. Sending me I did not even know what was going on.

Malik's mother called the ambulance. When it arrived, I refused to get in. I started walking toward Broad Street, Broad and Allegheny, to Temple University Hospital. I don't know what I was thinking—feeling embarrassed to get into the ambulance. That was really silly. Malik came running up behind me, asking, "Why didn't you get into the ambulance?" but I just kept walking. It was only a couple of blocks away.

When I got to the hospital, the nurse didn't even get a chance to triage me. It was really hard getting ready to have a baby by myself, with no one there. Malik wasn't even my child's father, and he had a girlfriend with his own child on the way. I went straight back to the delivery room, lay down, and the baby's head started to crown. That was an easy labor—he came out right away with only two pushes. Nobody was there with me, but I felt so alive. Happy, but sad.

The next day, my father came to see me, and then everyone else came after him. The first prince had arrived. Later, Malik's mother came to the hospital looking all geeked out on cocaine. Before I went to the hospital to have my son, I had hidden my package of drugs. But apparently, Malik's mother found it. I asked her what happened to it, and she was so high—she and her girlfriend acted like they were looking for it.

I wasn't stupid; I wasn't going to take it with me to the hospital, but I knew damn well what I did with it. She tried to play it off. She could have gotten me killed. She had an addiction and to her that's all that mattered at that time. I called the hoodlums I was selling for and told them what happened. They immediately questioned Malik's mother. She was acting all scared. They tried to intimidate me, but I had a messed-up life, a messed-up childhood—I got the s—— beat out of me every single day, so that s—— didn't work on me.

Eventually, they gave her another package to sell. I told her to work it off, and I was off the hook. So I stayed on Sixteenth and

Allegheny, taking care of my first place. My aunt would come over during the day to help me with the baby after she walked her daughter, my little cousin, to school.

After a while, I got tired of Malik sneaking around, seeing his baby momma and me on the side, so I started talking to my high school sweetheart, James. He would always come to my rescue, no matter what. I started going back and forth to my aunt's house on the weekends. She would babysit for me while I went out with James, like we used to do back when I was living in Carson Valley. That's why I always got into trouble. I'd leave during the weekend and come back like it was nothing, knowing I'd be put on restriction, but I didn't give a s———.

After I finished having fun with James on the weekend, I'd go back to Malik's mother's house on Sixteenth and Allegheny. I did this for several weeks. Eventually, Malik found out I was talking to James, thanks to his nosy sister—the one who loved stirring up confusion, like a jinn. She had nothing better to do than snitch.

One weekend, Malik came over to my aunt's house looking for me. He was crying because of what his sister told him about James and me hooking up again. I asked him, "What the hell are you worried about? You have a girlfriend."

So he played with me until I decided to go back with him to his mother's house on Sixteenth and Allegheny. Silly me again—I fell for the okey dokey. I returned with him, and when I got there, I noticed that my son's clothes were missing. He went and got them for me and said, "I was mad because I thought you were going to leave me, so I was going to throw the baby's things away since I found out you were talking to your high school sweetheart again."

I stayed on Sixteenth and Allegheny, taking care of my first prince. I knew how to take care of children from taking care of my sisters and brother, but I quickly realized that taking care of a newborn baby was totally different. I was really scared—my first prince kept throwing up his milk, and I didn't know what to do. My baby was getting really sick, and the doctors had given me the wrong milk. I tried to breastfeed him, but he became really sick, and his soft spot started to sink in from being dehydrated.

I finally took him to the hospital, and when I got there, the nurses and doctors checked him out. He was very dehydrated. The doctors told me that if I hadn't brought him in that day, he would have passed away. My baby stayed in the hospital for about a month, and I visited him every day. When I finally got to bring him home, they had changed his milk to something he could digest.

A couple of months later, I decided to take him to see his father's side of the family. When I first found out I was pregnant, I had left to try to better my situation. Nobody knew where I was. I just up and left, and I didn't start coming back around until I was about seven months pregnant. They were surprised and very happy to see me and my first prince. The grandmother even wanted to keep him for the weekend, so I left him with her and went back to Malik's mother's house.

Malik was very angry that I took the baby to see his father's side of the family. Malik had anger issues. He was still seeing his child's mother, but he got mad at me because I took my baby to see his family. I guess he thought I was going over there to see the father and get back with him or something. But that wasn't the case at all—I just wanted my child to see his grandmother and his family.

Eventually, I got tired of Malik and his sisters' b———, and I left. I started staying with a lady who lived up the street from my aunt, who lived on York Street. I was very unhappy there. The house lady said she wanted everybody in the house to give her all of their food stamps so she could go shopping, but she was full of mess. My son didn't have the things I usually bought for him, so I left and went up the street to stay with my aunt again.

It was a never-ending story with Malik and me hooking back up. We got back together months after I left with my baby, and then I got pregnant with my daughter. That's when I started getting depressed. I didn't have a stable living situation for me and my children. My first son's father started coming back around, so I stopped talking to Malik again, even though I was pregnant with his daughter.

I asked my son's grandmother if I could stay with her when I got closer to my due date, and she said yes. My son's grandmother was a very loving person, without a negative bone in her body. She took care of and accepted children who weren't even her biological grandchildren, and she helped anyone who needed her love.

On Friday nights, after work, she would get steamed shrimp and a bottle of Long Island iced tea, cook dinner for everybody, and we'd play spades all night. She would drink Long Island iced tea, but I didn't because I was pregnant with my daughter. Staying there was a good thing—no one argued, and there were no negative vibes.

I had my daughter, who was Malik's child. I was in the hospital for two weeks because she was trying to come too early. I finally called my daughter's grandmother's house to get in touch with Malik to let him know that our daughter was about to be born. He came up to Temple University, where I was going to deliver.

Malik seemed happy, knowing that he had his first daughter on the way—he only had a son with his other girlfriend. He came to the hospital with a yellow rose, visited for a couple of hours, and then left. The doctors kept giving me medication to stop the contractions and keep my daughter from coming too soon.

Days later, the doctors took fluid to test if my baby's lungs were developed enough for her to be born, as she was coming too soon, before the nine-month due date. The test results showed that my baby's lungs were developed enough. That same afternoon, my contractions started again. My baby was determined to come, and there was no stopping her.

I didn't have any pain medication, and the pain was excruciating. The doctor in the room just stood there, staring at me. I was crying and screaming for him to help me. I felt her head starting to come out, and I was terrified. Finally, the nurse came into the room and told me to push. I pushed so hard that my baby came out after just one push. I was exhausted and confused as to why the doctor had just stood there, looking at me with an evil expression.

After giving birth, I went back to my room to rest. No one came to see me. I felt so alone and depressed that I cried out of nowhere. I think I had a case of postpartum depression. Later that evening, the nurse brought my baby to the room. I looked at her—she was the most precious little baby girl I had ever seen. She came early, so she only weighed five pounds and thirteen ounces. Thank God there were no complications, and we only had to stay a couple of days.

My son's grandmother wasn't driving at the time, so she came on the bus to make sure we got home safely. She wasn't my biological grandmother, but that's just the kind of person she was—full of love, pure, and heaven- sent. She was a blessing not just to me but to everyone around her. She was a genuine human being, and everybody loved her. She definitely touched my heart. I always wondered why my mother couldn't have been like her.

It's always a gift when God puts someone like that into your life. When you don't have a woman figure to show you love or to teach you what it means to be a woman, people like my first son's grandmother, my fairy godmother, and my aunt become blessings. They didn't turn their backs on me.

I was taken advantage of when I was seventeen years old, while I was drunk and asleep. But it could have been worse—I could have been killed, like when I was in the drug game or robbing the wrong person. From personal experience, I believe and have learned that Allah (God) has a plan for everyone, and mine is to raise awareness for the irresponsible people who didn't help me and my siblings while we were in the clutches of a serial killer.

**BIRTH**
>   1976
>   Philadelphia, Philadelphia
>   County, Pennsylvania, USA

**DEATH**
>   Jul 1981 (aged 4–5)
>   Philadelphia, Philadelphia
>   County, Pennsylvania, USA

**BURIAL**
>   Burial Details Unknown

**MEMORIAL ID**
>   89020880

Aliyah Davis, The Girl In The Trunk, and her baby brother Saceed.

On February 12, 1982 two Pennsylvania Department of Transportation employees performing repairs on the western side of the Platt bridge, discovered remains of a young girl found inside a steamer trunk under the Platt Memorial Bridge in Philadelphia.

She turned out to be 5YO Aliyah Davis beaten to death by her stepfather in 1981, 7 months before her body was discovered.

Warrants were issued for The mother, Maria Davis Fox, and stepfather, Charles Fox, in their mid-30s, on an assortment of charges relating to the murder of Aliyah Davis and the repeated beatings of her brother and sister.

The mother was also charged with welfare fraud for collecting aid for the child after her July 1981 death.

A grand jury began probing the case about a month after the dead girl's sister, Amira Davis, told their natural father that she had watched the stepfather beat Aliyah to death with a stick at their home.

Amira Davis told grand jurors that her mother also watched the beating, but did nothing to stop it.

Amira Davis described how, when she was 8, she saw Fox beat his 5-year-old stepdaughter after she had a bowel movement in her clothes as the family had gathered to watch a television program, The Dukes of Hazzard, in their living room in the 4700 block of Baltimore Avenue.

"First he used his hand, and then he started beating her with a broomstick," she said.

"He hit her on her head and the sides of her head, then he banged her against the wall, picked her up and kicked her. . . . She was making whining noises.

Then she made kind of a groaning noise."

Amira testified that Fox placed Aliyah on a bed in the living room, where she lay for three days with Flies swarmed around the body.

On the fourth day, she said, her sister was gone, as was a steamer trunk that had been placed at her bedside.

Charles Fox's friend, Craig Butler, who was granted immunity from prosecution in exchange for his grand-jury testimony, told the panel that he saw Aliyah Davis lying on her back making gurgling noises one day in the summer of 1981 after Fox summoned him.

Fox, told him the child had bumped her head in the bathtub.

Neither stepfather nor mother sought any medical help, Butler said.

The next day, Fox asked his help to dump the body, explaining that he feared he might be charged with child abuse if he went to the authorities.

Butler said he borrowed a car and helped Fox dump the steamer trunk that contained the corpse.

The tiny body, its mouth stuffed with gauze, was found by workers seven months later, but remained unidentified for years.

Amira Davis and her 16-year-old brother, ████████, also told the grand jury that Charles Fox regularly beat them.

Both also said their mother assaulted them and had stabbed them in separate incidents.

Maria Davis Fox had been sentenced to 8 years probation for the death of one of her other children.

Police said that in September 1973, while Ronald and Maria Davis were married and living with their children in the 4400 block of North Cleveland Street in North Philadelphia, a rescue unit was dispatched to their home to investigate a medical emergency.

Paramedics found the couple's 17-month-old son, Saeed, in a second-floor bedroom.

The boy showed no signs of life and was pronounced dead minutes later at Temple University Hospital, police said.

The Medical Examiner's Office listed the cause of death as injuries to the head and body.

Police interviewed the parents and charged Maria Davis with murder and involuntary manslaughter. Ronald Davis was not charged.

The case went to court on June 10, 1974, and Maria Davis, who admitted to striking the boy, pleaded guilty to second-degree murder and involuntary manslaughter and was sentenced to eight years' probation, according to court records.

**Flowers • 225**

Rest in peace little one. You are safe now.

Left by <u>Rita Walker</u> on 24 Sep 2024
Toggle Flower Dropdown

# AMIRA DAVIS

Left by <u>Blessed\*Are\*Pure\*in\*Heart
.⁺·₊°♡°₊·⁺.</u> on 18 Sep 2024
Toggle Flower Dropdown

<u>Leave a Flower View All</u>

**See more Davis memorials in:**

- <u>Find a Grave</u>

<u>Flower Delivery</u>
**Explore more**
- Birth, Baptism & ChristeningSearch
- Marriage & DivorceSearch
- Death, Burial, Cemetery &
  ObituariesSearch

By Ancestry®
**SPONSORED BY
<u>FORGOTTEN ANGELS</u>**

IN MEMORY OF SAAID AND AALIYAH

Learn about sponsoring

- **Created by:** Forgotten Angels
- Added: Apr 23, 2012
- Find a Grave Memorial
  ID: 89020880

# About the Author

Amira Davis lived a very sheltered life and never played outside with other kids. She was abused every day by her mother and stepfather. They were fed closely and made sure the kids' hair were done and clean. She did chores and washed clothes by hand. She did not go to school until she was fourteen years old, but she was literate. They read books on their own when they could get the chance. Amira is a fifty-year-old who hasn't been through a lot in her life, and she is grateful that she made it out of situations that she was in all by herself. She believes she is a strong person, and she wants to raise awareness about her brother and sister and all the children that the Department of Human Services has failed.